**Why
God
Permits
Evil**

WORKS BY MILLER WILLIAMS

POETRY

A Circle of Stone
Recital (Spanish translation of *A Circle of Stone*,
    by Justo Uribe)
So Long at the Fair
The Only World There Is
Halfway from Hoxie
Why God Permits Evil

CRITICAL STUDIES

The Achievement of John Ciardi
The Poetry of John Crowe Ransom

WORKS TRANSLATED BY MILLER WILLIAMS

Poems and Antipoems of Nicanor Parra (with others)
Emergency Poems of Nicanor Parra

WORKS EDITED BY MILLER WILLIAMS

19 Poetas de Hoy en los EEUU
Southern Writing in the Sixties: Poetry
    (with John William Corrington)
Southern Writing in the Sixties: Fiction
    (with John William Corrington)
Chile: An Anthology of New Writing
    (edited and translated)
Contemporary Poetry in America
How Does a Poem Mean?
    (with John Ciardi)
Railroad: Trains and Train People in American Culture
    (with James Alan McPherson)

Why God Permits Evil

Poems by MILLER WILLIAMS

LOUISIANA STATE UNIVERSITY PRESS
Baton Rouge and London
1977

Designer: Albert Crochet
Type face: VIP Palatino
Typesetter: Graphic World, Inc., St. Louis, Missouri
Printer and binder: Kingsport Press, Kingsport, Tennessee

LIBRARY OF CONGRESS CATALOGING IN PUBLICATION DATA

Williams, Miller.
  Why God permits evil.

  I. Title.
PS3545.I53352W5   811'.5'4   77–8711
ISBN 0–8071–0377–2
ISBN 0–8071–0378–0 pbk.

Grateful acknowledgment is made to the editors of the following
publications in which some of these poems first appeared, some in
earlier forms: *Antabus, Back Door, Barataria Review, Cimarron Review,
Concerning Poetry, Ghent Quarterly, Mill Mountain Review, New Orleans
Review, Paintbrush, Poetry Now, Red Weather, Southern Poetry Review,
Southern Review,* and *Vanderbilt Poetry Review.*

Sections of "Notes from the Agent on Earth" first appeared in *Back
Door, Inlet, New Orleans Review,* and *Red Weather.*

"Getting Experience" has appeared in the anthology, *Traveling
America with Today's Poets* (Macmillan), edited by David Kherdian.

"Why God Permits Evil" was included in the Borestone Mountain
Poetry Awards volume *Best Poems of 1976.*

Thanks also, and especially, to Chet Biscardi.

For Judith and John Ciardi

Contents

Why
God
Permits
Evil

Everyone Dies in a Light Rain

lying on the highway
surrounded by strangers

This is what the Oxford English
Dictionary tells us
the Atlanta Constitution tells us
and the World Almanac
and the girl at the counter
in the Frank and Louise Cafe

This is what
the telephone number
in the toilet stall
tells us
The rodeo rider
holding the rope in one hand
the horse an arc beneath him
the other hand floating
tells us again
The white telephone
by the white bed
in the round room
tells us again

as also the inverted car
tells us
cars and pickup trucks pulling off and idling
on the slick shoulder
anybody hurt
and then someone waving the traffic on
the arm repeating its small important circle
as proud as anarchy
ordained as law
as we edge obediently by the cold radiant place

and drive a while without saying anything
as if we were turning something
over in our minds

Potter, Vidalia

Vidalia Potter (who often as not
put sheet to show and quilt underneath
when she made the bed and always forgot

the social worker woman's name
and made coffee that went to waste
every time the woman came,

who fretted about a festering sore
on one of the legs of one of the girls
and walked at six to the Safeway store

for bottle drinks—Dr. Pepper,
Strawberry Creme, a 7 Up—
bread and sliced bologna for supper,

who never was sick and never was well,
whose man had a job at the chicken plant
and told time by the quitting bell,

who loved her children as best she could
and washed the leg and swept the floor
sometimes and thought about the good

strong-smelling man who called her to bed
when he wasn't drunk and he wasn't tired)
never could get it fixed in her head
what the social worker said.

Everything Is Fine Here How Are You

She blinks above her sunglasses at the man
putting the letters up on the movie marquee.
Along the wire he slides an S, an N.
His sleeves are cut away. The marguerita
she presses against her mouth. She feels her mouth
suck in against the salt. She watches the man
test his way descending the step ladder
and jerk it spraddled across the sidewalk.
The sound has her in front of a shingled house,
her mother pushing the screendoor open, calling
always. She watches him climb the ladder again.
If she passes that way and speaks to him
he will go off and leave her in a grove of oaks,
the twisted bra knotted about her wrists,
the panties stuffed in her mouth, the eyes
her own eyes paying no attention.

Reading the Arkansas Gazette on Microfilm

I let it go for the fact of it fast as it will
pages and days sliding by in a gray blur
black spaces falling before the headlines
marking the nights and mornings until I can tell
Sundays by their length and the running colors
department store ads from news from real estate
by normal sequence and shifting densities.
I almost wonder if I watched it long enough,
could I tell the car wrecks from the weddings,
weddings from rapes and fires and book reviews.
The names in accidents and baseball scores
for months pass by in minutes. I see
that I have stayed from April into autumn
and think of a mind that saw it all go by
as fast as that in the first place and wonder at it.

The Unknown Sailor

Sits up in bed in his navy robe
and looks at the wall or whatever moves
between his bed and the wall and neither
approves nor disapproves.

No one knows his name or his town
or even his country. In forty-four
a hospital ship in Boston harbor
put him ashore

with the label Navy and nothing else.
For those thin years he has never spoken.
He smiles and blinks in a white silence
occasionally broken

by wives and sons and daughters and friends
of men who went to war and were lost
and never found. They leave with another
sailor crossed—

or soldier, merchant marine or marine—
from a nameless list. Be grateful for that.
Here in the ward he may have an inkling
of where he's at.

Those lives he moved among before
have long since filled the space and the town
has closed the way the sea closes
if ships go down.

Where To Turn When Sorrow Comes
Like a Black Bull in Your Dreams

Start with the house: the smell of the person dead
heavy and vaguely accusing and then gone;
bedpillow, shoes and hat and preferred chair
like half-domesticated animals
finding their first ways.

                    Start with the death;
friends coming with ancient platters; the altered kin
entering rooms as quietly as spies,
whispering comfort like a dangerous secret;
the journey behind the hearse, with every word
irrelevant and thin, and all the faces
around the grave turned off and folded down.
Then home again, where as if a train
began to move, the closed and numbered days
bump past going gradually faster.

                    Start with the signs.
Pain in the chest. Headaches. Bad dreams.
The reaming finger with its little condum;
the apologetic needle; the sphygmomanometer,
its one egg panting in the doctor's palm;
the x-ray's nostrils sniffing into places
invisibly scarlet. Each one having the right,
they wait behind their warrants with long words
for any person whose name is inscribed there
to sit or stand up or stop to count change
or stop the car in line at a traffic light
or lean forward to reach for the radio.

Begin with beginnings: a man and a woman lie down.
It all becomes right, abstract and natural.

But Death is a robber. Death is a son of a bitch.

Go back to the grave and stand, crying like a child.

For Fred Carpenter Who Died in His Sleep

Penniless to our surprise
at the peak of his earning power he lies:
a man of the mean, who rarely meant
much harm, and nearly always spent
his money wisely; who got his views
from *Newsweek* and *U.S. News*
(though he only trusted the latter)
and wondered constantly what was the matter
with those there was something the matter with
(some of those being his kin and kith)
and believed what was right or discreetly done
was right, and looked for a little fun
when he traveled out of town
and wished his woman would go down
but she never would.
He understood.

On Hearing About the Death of Mitzi Mayfair

Hurrah for the next
man that dies
said Errol Flynn
and someone
snuk open the earth
and let him in.

Jesus died legend has it on dogwood
whose blossom for that reason
cursed itself into a cross.
The small red spot
at the tip of each plain petal
spread just at the Easter season
we say is the blood but it isn't.
You know it's not.

I close my eyes and see a calendar
with a date circled in red.

The trouble is that
my madness
was not the other half
of your madness.

There has never been a poem
to explain anything.
For that reason
many people who would otherwise
write poems do not.
Praise such people.

On the Way Home from Nowhere, New Year's Eve

For papers I think I need, we bump off
the street and stop. I leave the engine on,
mean to make my way to the buzzing light
above the back door, but the door is dark.
Old Main's a hulking, dull, uncertain form,
no windows and no size. Then I remember

one small truth I didn't mean to remember,
that all the lights at ten would be turned off
for somebody's purpose. I enter the hollow form,
try one time to flick the light switch on
and shrug my way into the seamless dark.
What outside seemed scattered, useless light

would be a brilliance here. Reflections. Moonlight.
Sensing my way between the walls I remember
old mythologies of daytime and the dark
spun by gods and monster movies, cast off
with ignorance. My fingers stumble on
another switch. Nothing. I feel my form

falling away into another form.
I hear the hound, look for the quick light
glancing out of his eyes and imagine my own
open, aimless, milky. I remember
what children think of when the lights are off.
Something brushing the hand. To fit the dark

I tell myself I am blind. In such a dark
I could be moving down the spaceless form
of time, a painted tunnel. I twist off
my shoes and walk in deafness. Leap. Grow light
for one slow moment, then loose parts remember
gravity. I twist the sounds back on.

I'm over a million years old and going on
thirteen. I've always been afraid of the dark.
There truly are warlocks, witches, and I remember
banshees, saints and the always shifting form
of Satan himself. I feel a fly light
and crawl across my forehead. I brush it off.

Going on, I grab some papers off
some desk in the dark and turn back toward the light
I barely remember, running, hungry for form.

A Dialectic on Science and Religion

What fact is fact?
We began as a line so thin a fly
if there had been one then would not have seen us
gathering like small tribes toward that first
civilization we have come to call
the virus

which is our best honest and common name
the simple source of all three-sided things
in whose computed corners all creatures are joined
by that gray nature whose unmind is measure
whose rage is ratio.
So we are told.

Although they also say
we are the imaginings of imagined gods
who thereby continually conceive us.
What fact is fact?

Of which gods then beware.
There is some rumor and reason to suspect
they do plan to fall one day upon us,
opening every door and walking in,
old math teachers to insult us
into splintery floors,
smiling employers to straighten our ties
and fire us.

Twelve Months Again for Joy:
Prayer for a Broke Anniversary

Lord. Father. Sir.
A life of lucre and liquor and love
is what I still prefer
if these can come together. If not
well then I'm happy with her
for little is money alone I know
and less is alcohol.
Still we've had reason to believe
you have the wherewithal
and things are counted best by threes.
As you recall.

Footnote on the Invention of Small Pleasures

Young Adam surely must
being newly from dust
the only human life
and with no word for wife
have been somewhat perplexed
to find himself so sexed.

Speeding Past the I-40 Exit to Bascum
He Begins To Think About Tackett's Station
and Western Civilization and Peggy Hooper

Where the Woodrow Wilson School was once
squat blocks of pastel siding
slap back at the sun.

Why should it be there? Who was Woodrow Wilson?

We had a Dodge. When we hit a chicken
we had chicken.

Milton Tackett fixed tires and sold the rubbers
you had to have in your wallet
like a badge.
You're under arrest. Take off all your clothes.

Milton gave a package of rubbers free
for any pair of panties.
When you told him her name and he believed you
you got a dozen.
No sir I said I guess not.
Well he said if I said
pussy I could have one anyway.

A woman off the Titanic
talked Sunday night.
She said that all she heard them play
was a waltz.

I bought a Nash
for 97 dollars.
Sunday afternoons
cotton rows running up to the road
flicked by like spokes.
The cropdusting plane put down its pattern
back and forth across the field
like a shuttle.
I was drunk on speed

and metaphor. The world
was a weaving machine.

But on the other hand
said Alexander the Great
bringing down the sword on the Gordian knot
fuck fate

Didn't you used to live here?

Don't do that you're going to tear something
Look if I take off my clothes will it make you happy

I'm sorry. What did you say?

Nothing. Never mind.

Picker

Uvalde Texas to Nashville Tennessee
is near as a tavern jukebox, is twice as far
as Jesus to Judas, as a rusty Plymouth car
to a bus with a bedroom. We look outside to see

hundreds come honking to listen to whistle to praise
the picker among us, come to tell us again
about the differences, as mostly between
how we imagine marriage those quick days

till we do marry, and how we learn to live
together after with the debts and beer
and strangers' crotches open everywhere.
I watch to learn the life you learn to give

to tell the love and sickness in our skin
and neon lights and darkness. Lord we crave
those words for hardness of our bones, to save
the soul from puffiness. You put us in

flat touch with what we are, and make that touch
bearable first, then almost pleasant and then
plain necessary, how we try to mend
our nervous ways for nothing and drink too much

and want bad love. I listen to you sing
while lean red faces eat you up alive
to know by what bright secrets we survive
the flesh's soft transgressions. No rhyming thing

will give the sense men want of who they are.
Or undo the differences we didn't mean
to deal with once—as for instance between
the bus with the bedroom and the rusty car.

Which is a green distance and does grow
while the car in the side mirror shrinks away
and you want to touch the driver's shoulder and say
Man, we're going too fast. You don't though.

Prison

Past Mobile Home Estates

Past the Pentecostal Campgrounds

Past a barn
its roof lying beside it

a shack of unpainted planks
in a soybean field
an empty houseboat rotting in a green river

A cropdusting biplane set down by the highway ahead
turns itself into an irrigation pump
when the car gets close

You turn off 65 on the prison road.
There are hundreds of reasons for being on 65
but not for being on the prison road.
You feel somebody shifting inside of you
pushing your parts around. You believe it now.
This is where it starts.

Whites for the short hairs. They don't fit.
Tough shit. Go tell the boss
you quit.
What you do is fit the clothes.
Hands at your sides in single rows.
Don't touch the wall
unless you want to wash the hall
with your tongue and your piss and a bar of soap.
You will behave and be well. We hope.
You will bear in mind, if we rankle you some,
nobody here asked you to come.

What is there to say?
There may

be some small difference in one day
and the next and the next but there's no way
to name the difference, like a lay
in some whorehouse wherein they
all have the same look when you pay
only they never mean you to stay.
Except for this, what's there to say?

Some days there is a settling into the tomb.
Some nights there come whole years a man forgets
his wife and children and his unpaid debts
and prays for wet dreams and a bad sense of time.

Dear friend: She runs around. A friend.

Lord I want to go home, which is a small town
where I live with a lady who surely goes out
but would not let another man lie down
between the long legs that I dream about.

You stay yourself in a world of your mind's making.
Bones is the only man ever sent to jail
for buggery with a banty rooster. They tell
how they brought him to court with the swollen chicken
still stuck on, flapping its wings and squawking.

Ten years and mercy and a thin smile
before the board and after a little while
the gate opens and you feel your guts
pull tight and you go out and the gate shuts
and what you feel then is sharply the same
as that white fear you felt the day you came.
There will be a job. And a woman. And a telephone.
But first you will rent a room. And be drunk. And alone.

But flat time friend is ten years.
But even that friend disappears
day by day though days grow long
when nights are short and walls are strong
and food is flat and beds are hard
and there's a meanness in every guard
and the family coming to bring you cheer
grows a little stranger year by year.

For a Young Woman Who Always Looked Where She Was Going

Great beauty can get so close to deformity
the difference disappears in the wrong light.
Then roundness turns into enormity,
grace settles into sweetness and that slight
cast to the shoulder suddenly seems affliction,
the neck a cylinder, the mouth a well,
the teeth, bones; truth twists into fiction,
clever repeats to dumb, home to hotel.

Careful and dead, how could you have seen
those uncertain distinctions and stumbled across
the purely natural line. Woman, between
what you were and are is the dark and only
mark not drawn by us.
And I am peeved and lonely.

For a Friend Who Comes to Mind
at Three in the Morning

This place where love began
is diminished as much
as Bill Sloane was a man.

Well, as you would have said,
It's finished as such.
Meaning Hell, I'm dead.

We talked and drank one night
a while till dawn;
you told Jim Beam and me
There'll come a time you might

happen together, you two,
when I'll be gone.
Toast him that used to be.
So. Now you are. So now we do.

It's Hard To Think the Brain

a ball of ropey dough
should have invented pain
or come to know

how there are things we lend
a fragile credence to
and hope to comprehend
but never do.

Watching a Movie Made in New Orleans

I see a trolley back slowly past a woman
sitting beside the tracks
and see the woman
flip in front of the trolley when it passes
look after it frozen in fear and lie down on the tracks.

What are they doing
Now they speed it up and run it backwards

Suddenly I understand the loaves and fishes
healing the blind man
Lazarus
the whole thing.

The Jesus Woman Standing at My Door

came with a bible in the middle of what I do
How are things in Porlock I asked her
No she said I'm from Joplin Missouri

In Love in Ovid's Lounge at 3 P.M.

He knows the right wines in this flickering place.
She has in candlelight a perfect face.
Harry would never know her. Nor Emma him.

On Hearing the President Talk About Defense

The drains have filled with fine ash drifting down
so long it's hardly noticed anymore.
He buys a lot and builds a house in town
and spells out *cave canem* on the floor.

A Polemic Poem About the End of the Democratic Dream

Everything will be as simple as cement.
Everything will be duller than the Yellow Pages.
Everything will make more sense than mail boxes.
Like stacks of folding chairs, everything is ready.

After You Die You Don't Give a Piddling Damn

I do Lord, I do. Therefore I am.

Memphis, 2 P.M.

I saw a woman getting out of a car.
She said to the man in the car
leave me alone.
She closed the door with both hands.
She said to the man please
just leave me alone.

It was a new Plymouth,
blue with a white top.

Why I Go to Roger's Pool Hall

Pitcher I talked to told me he doesn't much like
to strike a man out if he's barely hanging on.
Every time I send him back to the benches
I help make up the manager's mind to cut him.
You think he thinks that every time he connects
he drops my chances of getting called to Atlanta?
Well I said I don't know. I never played baseball.

How To Stop Smoking

If you are a man
think of a woman wiggling out of her underwear
saying come on you don't have to love me.

If you are a woman
think of the man thinking that.

Practice. Practice

And Then I Headed on Back Home

I went to New York and went to the poet's address
Four flights up in a building with clean windows
He asked what I wanted without opening the door
I told him I liked his poems and came to say so
He said if that's true I thank you very much
I told him his milk was out there getting warm

A Car Rolls Off the Road in Front of Me

A girl crawls out of the overturned car.
I see that she isn't hurt.
She can't find her cat.

The woman with the first aid kit
goes back to her car.
The truck driver and the farmer go back to their trucks.
All the people go back to start their motors,
some saying Thank God, others saying She really was lucky.

She says What do I do now.
I promise to call the police at the next town.
I tell my wife about it when I get home.
I tell her the girl had an interesting face.

She knows what I mean.

A Game of Marbles

Back in the town I used to live in
I see some boys shooting marbles
in the same empty lot.

One of them shifting on his haunches
looks up and sees me.

WW I

Still we turn a corner and there it is—
the trenches, the green gas,
the helmets like hubcaps,
the bombs small enough for a man
to die alone in,
the mademoiselle from Armenteers, the mud,
those square little planes like canvas boxkites.
What is it we keep trying to remember?
Wilfred Owen died. That wasn't it.
Long lines who never heard of Wilfred Owen
synchronize their watches and crawl under barbed wire
looking for something
maybe a map,
a canteen with brandy still in it.
And what would brandy taste like
after all that time.
Good. It tastes good.

Husband

She's late. He mixes another drink.
He turns on the television and watches
a woman kissing the wrong man.
He looks at his watch. He feels close
to the cat. Well Cat, he says.
He feels foolish.
He mixes another drink and stands
turning the stem of the glass
back and forth in his fingers.
This also makes him feel foolish.
He looks at his watch. Well Cat, he says.
Lights turn into the driveway.
He slumps into his chair. He
kicks off his shoes and spreads
the open newspaper peacefully
over his face.
He hears the tiny grating of the key.
His heart knocks to get out.

How Does a Madsong Know That's What It Is?

If vampires do suck blood, if space is time,
if there is a hell for sins and heaven for virtues,
if the dead do remember, if once witches
did visit with the devil and did come
to Massachusetts when the devil came,
if matter turns to light as it approaches
the speed of light it therefore never reaches,
if Tanna leaves lead home, or the pentogram,
all these are carnival tricks. What is a ghost,
a resurrection, a warp in time, a hell,
beside the fact that we do seem to exist?
What idiot believes in anything?
What idiot is there who doesn't believe it all
With heigh! The sweet birds! Oh, how they sing!

The Science of Life

You can in the first place
not be born

failing that
you can be buried
or be cremated
give your body up for bone
skin organ various tissue
transplants
be stuffed
go down in water and never be found
die in the desert and be eaten
by small animals
or failing all these
live forever

So What?

The lilacs are gone too
and so are the falcons
whole species genera families
disappeared
and the albatross
gone too
and the groundhog
the nightingale raven birch
all of them done for
and every dappled thing.

Apeneck Sweeney got among nightingales
but they were stuffed.

So you came to a bad end.
What do I do?
So I walk out under a dark marquee.
Should I walk back and forth upon the earth
sidewalk blacktop and gravel
listening for some word
not certainly mine
of you as you were,
some possible sign then
of such tree or flower
such beast or such a bird?

All of you died.
But we are used to death.
Sic transit gloria mundi
A Kempis said
or something like that like screw
like so what am I supposed to say
though I do love you
and did.

What Opus What New World Ode What Dickory Dock What Image or Two Lines Run Together or Two Words Will Outlast Long or Deserve To the Track of Light Where Two Lives Ran Together or One Good Poet Found a Simple Way Across a Page

We do cut our initials everywhere,
on walls of falling buildings, in dying trees,
make friends and name our children carefully,
write letters we intend to have collected,
make being out of fashion fashionable,
publish what we do in the good places,
die with our numbered worksheets in fireproof files.
Or certain we are one with the universe,
leave nothing but a generous name and year,
words of revelation and legends well-built.

Flat-eyed miscast romantics, two-fingered magicians.
No one will know in a hundred and fifty years
nor ought to, nor a hundred for most of us,
what we did or why except a few
looking after the final degrees in dullness.

We have failed at what makers of poems do,
which was never to save the world from the world
but to save the world from the failure of poetry.

The fact is people in prison are brutalized
and doctors live off sickness and preachers off guilt
and poets live off love. And guilt and sickness
and death and death in war especially.
None of which facts we have gotten our words around,
not having understood them, words or facts.
We have been sure and courageous and skillfully wrong.

Well somebody says to you how do you know
the difference between a musical note and November,
if God was a fire at 14 Palmyra Street
or a 1928 penny or only a lesbian.
Well you think what do you do with that.

You see you get to a point where you can't tell.

The Inmate from the State Hospital
Tells His Hostage
How He Was Told To Talk Plain

I was not fooled.
For all their trying to be like me
like us
I knew they were lying.
Oh they were good though. They said dear friend
we are all of us sealed in this house
and we must reason together.
Oh they were good
for in the eyes they did look also wild.
They beat upon my head and heart. They said
plain talk is honest art.
It does not do for counting children out
and so is true thereby.
Shit they do lie.
Nothing is truer than rhyme.
Rhymes signify.
Come here Sweet Child.

He Notices One Morning
How She Has Changed Again
As It Were Overnight

That's twice.

Where do you people come from?
Where do you go?
Conversations get cut off in the middle.
Hello. Already I miss her.
The way you get out of bed though.

They won't ever come back even at night.

Who wants them to.
They were good women. Let them go.

Someday you and I may think at the same time
of a restaurant in San Francisco or Tucson
and they will run into one another there
and not be surprised.

Why God Permits Evil:
For Answers to This Question
of Interest to Many
Write Bible Answers Dept. E–7

—ad on a matchbook cover

Of interest to John Calvin and Thomas Aquinas
for instance and Job for instance who never got

one straight answer but only his cattle back.
With interest, which is something, but certainly not

any kind of answer unless you ask
God if God can demonstrate God's power

and God's glory, which is not a question.
You should all be living at this hour.

You had Servetus to burn, the elect to count,
bad eyes and the Institutes to write;

you had the exercises and had Latin,
the hard bunk and the solitary night;

you had the neighbors to listen to and your woman
yelling at you to curse God and die.

Some of this to be on the right side;
some of it to ask in passing, Why?

Why badness makes its way in a world He made?
How come he looked for twelve and got eleven?

You had the faith and looked for love, stood pain,
learned patience and little else. We have E–7.

Churches may be shut down everywhere,
half-written philosophy books be tossed away.

Some place on the south side of Chicago
a lady with wrinkled hose and a small gray

bun of hair sits straight with her knees together
behind a teacher's desk on the third floor

of an old shirt factory, bankrupt and abandoned
except for this just cause, and on the door:

Dept. E–7. She opens the letters
asking why God permits it and sends a brown

plain envelope to each return address.
But she is not alone. All up and down

the thin and creaking corridors are doors
and desks behind them: E–6, E–5, 4, 3.

A desk for every question, for how we rise
blown up and burned, for how the will is free,

for when is Armageddon, for whether dogs
have souls or not and on and on. On

beyond the alphabet and possible numbers
where cross-legged, naked and alone,

there sits a pale, tall and long-haired woman
upon a cushion of fleece and eiderdown

holding in one hand a hand-written answer,
holding in the other hand a brown

plain envelope. On either side, cobwebbed
and empty baskets sitting on the floor

say *in* and *out*. There is no sound in the room.
There is no knob on the door. Or there is no door.

The Friend

I hadn't seen him in twelve years.
He could put his hands between the wall
and a light and make a rollercoaster
a kidney machine a split T
running a double reverse.
I heard he was in town so of course I invited him.
I took down a picture to have a blank space
on the wall.
Everyone gathered in a semicircle.
I turned off all the lights except one lamp.
Go ahead I said.
He made a dog.
Then he made a rabbit. It only had one ear.
The elephant didn't have a trunk
and looked like a cow.
Jesus Christ I said What happened.
I could hear someone across the room
mixing a drink in the dark.

Getting Experience

The first real job I had was delivering drugs
for Jarman's Pharmacy in Bascum, Arkansas.

If everyone was busy or in the back I sold things.
A cloudy woman with pentecostal hair

softly asked for sanitary napkins.
She brought the Kleenex back unwrapped in twenty minutes.

Shame said Mr. Jarman, we shouldn't make a joke
of that and made me say I'm sorry and fired me.

When I found out what the woman wanted
I had to say I did what everyone said I did.

That or let them know I hadn't heard of Kotex.
Better be thought bad than known for stupid.

The first hard fight I had was after school
with Taylor Wardlow West in Bascum, Arkansas.

Ward West chased me home from school when I was lucky.
My father said Ward West was insecure.

Go smile at him he said and let him know
you mean to be his friend. My father believed in love.

All day I smiled and twisted in my seat to see him
all hate and slump by himself in the back of the room.

After school he sat on my chest and hit me
and then his little brother sat on my chest and hit me.

And then his little sister sat on my chest and hit me.
She made me so ashamed I tried to kick her

and kicked Ward West in the face. When he could see
I was rounding the corner for home. Jesus, Jesus, Jesus.

Next day everybody told me over and over
how I had balls to make those stupid faces,

him the son of a bitch of the whole school
and how I surely did kick the piss out of him.

Ward had to go to the dentist. Also his father beat him.
He didn't come to school for two days.

Then he left me alone. He said I was crazy.
Everybody thought I was a little crazy.

Although with balls. I just let them say I was.
Better be thought mad than known for stupid.

Sneeze, belch or fart. Choose if you have a choice.
Nobody's going to think you're good and sane and smart.

Walking Past a Parked Car You Suddenly Stop But

the girl changing her clothes in the backseat
is not really there.
It's only a quilt
folded up
a bag of groceries a six pack
a flaw in the glass.
You might as well go on wherever you were going.

Being Here

The ring of a doorbell
at three in the morning
even before you know who's standing out there
changes not only the face that flies into your head
but shoes also and the backs of chairs and the repetitions
of wallpaper.
You may say a quick prayer
but anyway you will take it as you have to.

Notes from the Agent on Earth: How To Be Human

In St. Peter's basilica in the City of Rome
there sits a holy father fashioned in marble
encircled by faces well-proportioned and doubtless.
His name is Gregory; he spoke for God.
He sits upon a slab; under that slab
the devil, winged and dog-faced, cat-pawed and crooked,
turns in his agony and bares his teeth,
bares his broken claws, turns his nostrils
almost inside out. The statue is his.
One purchases with popes and attendant angels
the privilege of discovering such a devil.
No one could dare to show him by himself.
This loser, this bad and living dream, this Lucifer
alone is more than all the hovering others.
Because he carries folded into his face
what no face erased in heaven carries,
the fear and loneliness to make us human.
All there is to understand is there.
None here has anything to share with angels.
What makes a human human (more than speech,
a pair of opposable thumbs or the set of the head)
is a cold hand that reaches from under the bed
and closes on your ankle; is lying awake
flat on your back in bed and becoming aware
your hands are coffin-crossed upon your chest,
not having the little courage to leave them there.
And the girl in the hotel lobby, lost in her fat,
forgetting the room of the man who likes her like that.
The woman with buttons on her back undone
to show she doesn't live with anyone.
Think of men and women in nursing homes.
These were senators, some of them, and bankers,
presidents of colleges, detectives,
people who passed laws, wrote books,
gave loans, found clues, presided over professors,

crying all night in thin metal beds for their mothers,
calling in high voices daddy daddy,
and mother and daddy dead for thirty years.

What we have in common and what we know
from Loneliness and Fear, called Adam and Eve,
and all we have to turn our hands to
are Love, Ambition, Faith, the Sense of Death.

Love is Fear and Loneliness fed and sleeping;
Faith is Fear and Loneliness explained,
denied and dealt in; Ambition which is envy
is Fear and Loneliness coming up to get you;
Death is Fear and Loneliness fading out.
This is the stuff of life and the gospel of art.
So art and life are much alike in this.
But art, because we see both ends, can please us.
We never know if life is a cave or a tunnel.
We only know we spend the days going deeper,
half in fucking or hunting flesh to fuck
and half philosophizing the fuck away
with talk about the nature of good and evil,
which is a waste of energy and time.
The only question with any answer that matters
is whether we have a little free will or none.

But this is only content; this is stuffing.
Flesh is distastefully still and marble is rock
without the patterns a body pushes through.
So life and art are much alike in this.
Life is change that finds a changing pattern,
says the pither of frogs and cat-slitter;
art is change we put a pattern to.
And so is sport and war and merchandising.
There is a difference but it doesn't matter.

The old nun who believes in nothing
crosses herself sitting down to supper
and men and women living in New Orleans
dress in the brown and orange clothes of autumn
one certain heavy, indistinguishable day.
They call this The First Day Of Autumn.
Some women in Messina whose times of mourning
come close together and touch and overlap
wear black into black the last ten years of their lives.

This is about Love and how to tell it.
Charles Hammond Walker of South Carolina,
son of Charles and Sue born Sue Ella Hammond,
daughter of Colonel John and Martha Hammond
of Tennessee got off a plane in Chicago
and got a taxi and got a hotel room
and got a badge and got a daily paper
and went to a movie house that shows movies
of naked people doing reciprocal things,
remembered when he got inside the movie
to put the plastic badge that had the name
Charles Hammond Walker in his pocket,
sat down and spread the paper across his lap,
took his penis and pulled it out of his pants
into the cool air. Charles Hammond Walker
has a wife who sometimes in South Carolina
goes dreaming up a chance, a quick chance.

There are many stories of contented lovers.
Some people believe them; be careful of these.
The best counsel is likely of no account.

One says: I love you and you alone. One says:
I have something to tell you. Please sit down.

This is about Faith and how to tell it.
Think if you saw a ghost you knew was a ghost.
All the questions answered by that knowledge
are questions of Faith, though this defeats the question.
Faith justified by fact is no faith.

Newspapers, no matter how final the news is,
invite subscriptions, which—though business—
is an act of faith in delay, in possibly not.

One says: The Lord is with us. One says:
There is a fountain filled with blood. Amen.

This is about the Will to Power, Envy,
Covetousness, Ambition, maker of popes,
wars, weddings, poems, and county fairs.

A private holding a microphone like a scepter
can bring commanding generals to silence.

Or start with the swollen moment, the blimp saying yes,
the drum major pumping like a piston,
the majorettes spinning their silver spokes,
pulling the band behind them, dividing the crowd;
cables connecting vans to high windows
cameras scanning the street. Look at the man
putting money into the parking meter.
Watch how the meter runs down, watch how the band

puts down its instruments and disappears,
how the vans pull away, look how the broken cables
go leaping behind them, look how the people leave,
the last ones on the last bus standing silent.
Look at the man with his hand on the parking meter.
Look at his shoulder, slick with pigeon drippings.
Watch how the pigeons fly away and come back.

Say some people are tourists. They go to Pompei.
They are unhappy there. They frequently stumble.
Back in the bus they sit astonished and grieve.
It's hard to believe, Well it's hard to believe.
They are not grieving for Pompei.

One says: He slipped away in the night. One says:
Everybody move up to the next desk.

This is about Death and how to tell it.

When a man looks down at the back of his hand
and sees the hand of his father he knows he is dying.

One says: Listen. When I was very young
my father took me out to see the mountains.
We renamed all the animals we saw
with words no one had ever put together
and then we forgot them. My father is long dead.

Much that is said of the dead is bullshit.

One says: Listen. It gets sweet close to the end.
It is very important not to be dead.

The eyes of people in the last hours are bright.

The Lord giveth, the Lord taketh away.
One says: Please Lord. And so much for that.

This is also something about Ambition.
Also Love. And Faith also. And Death.

A man who had too much to calculate
had a vision of hell, was afraid of the dark,
knew that he had walked in evil ways,
corrected his wife to death and darkened his children;
had done things besides unspeakably bad
and could not honestly ask for God's forgiveness
as he was only afraid and could never say
I'm sorry, Lord. He wanted such redemption
as wipes a life not clean but wipes it away.
And thought that he could have it. He spent his means
for fifteen years of the best brains to be had
in mathematics, space-time and madness
and had him when he was eighty by god
a simple time-machine, which ought not now
bend any imagination out of shape;
went back seventy years to the same town
and found himself at ten delivering papers;
stole the one car there was and ran himself down;
left himself across a wooden sidewalk,
who barely lied to his mother or masturbated,
and went directly to heaven if any can.
He could not be the man who killed the boy
because he never lived to be the man,
having died at ten delivering papers,
survived by his parents, grieved by the fifth grade,
the first death by car in the whole county,
killed by a runaway Ford with no driver
of if a driver, none to be found.

There is much that matters. What matters most is survival.
What matters most in survival is learning the names
of things and the names of visions. If the horizon
for an example were real someone could go there
and call back to the rest of us and say
Here we are standing on the horizon.
But he would see that his friends were standing on it.
No sense of space or time is dependable here.
The difference in time is that we glance back
at those who stayed in time and didn't come with us,
and see ourselves still back there talking to them.
These are illusions, or seem to be illusions.
Leave them alone. What matters most is survival.

One says: Fuck you, Jack. One says: Up yours.
Climb on that and rotate, motherfucker.
Why can't I go? Everybody's going.
I didn't hardly touch you for godsake.

Be careful of too much imagination.
This attracts attention. Attention is trouble.
You have to develop competence, of course.
You have to think of doors opening toward you.
Take any pleasure in it and sooner or later
someone will notice your eyes have an absent look.
Someone with a glass in her hand will stop talking
and wait for you to answer. Practice caution.
Tell stories at parties the way you hear them.

Be careful of how the night moves into morning.
When things have gone right the day opens and closes,
one calendar square checked off and done with.
When something is wrong, when you've drunk too much

or had a fight over love or lost money,
the night runs into the morning in sick streaks
like the fluids of a dog run over in the last block.

Be careful of uniforms of any color,
of glass doors with initials painted on them,
of people always willing to go last.
Be careful of workers who have their own desks.
Be very careful of people whose young are hungry
and have large faces, of days set aside
for the celebration of national independence,
of those who are neither lonely nor afraid.

Be careful everywhere. This is a world—
what?—divided. Not as they say divided.
Think of this: running around the planet,
along the equator exactly, an iron fence;
half the population of the planet
stands on either side and shakes the bars
screaming to be let out, to be let in.